Roll of Th[...]
Hear My Cry

Mildred Delois Taylor

Guide written by Stewart Martin

C000177465

A *Letts* Literature Guide for GCSE

Contents

Contents

Plot summary

1 The story is set in 1930s' Mississippi, in the Deep South of America and covers about a year in the life of the Logan family. The Logans are a respectable black family who are much resented, especially by local white landowners, because they own 200 acres of their own land and are in the process of buying another 200.

4 Cassie and her three brothers help their grandmother, Big Ma, and their mother to farm cotton on their land. Cassie's experiences tell us a great deal about what it was like to live as a black family at that time, and we see her mature rapidly as she learns about the cruel ways of the world around her.

2 Racial tension runs high in the locality, fuelled mostly by the prejudice of a few white families who feel threatened by any attempt by the local black farming families to make their way in life. These local whites still see a white man's world in which 'niggers' should know their place as inferiors.

3  The story is told through the eyes of the young Cassie Logan, whose mother teaches at the local all-black school and whose father works away on the railroad for much of each year to earn the money they need.

12  T.J.'s white 'friends' involve him in the robbery of a store, during which a white man is killed and his wife beaten. The night men track down T.J. after he is blamed. The night men threaten to hang T.J., as well as Papa and Mr Morrison, but Papa starts a fire in order to stop the mob. Even so, it seems certain to Cassie – who has matured considerably by now – that T.J. will hang for a crime he did not commit.

11 The bank suddenly calls in the Logans' loan on the land. The family are rescued by Uncle Hammer, who sells his car and other possessions to raise the money.

Plot summary

5 The state will not allow blacks to attend the well-equipped all-white school and the Logan children are humiliated daily by its bus which threatens their lives and covers them with dust and mud. Eventually the children manage to disable the bus, so that the white children also have to walk to school.

7

The children's father, Papa, returns home and brings his friend, the powerfully built Mr Morrison, to stay with the family and protect them while he is away.

6 Cassie and her brother protest at being given books which have labels inside showing that the books have been discarded by white students. Their mother, who is regarded as a liberal by the other black teachers, attempts to remedy the situation by pasting paper over the offending pages. She is sacked when a black student called T.J., whom she catches cheating in a test, reports her actions to the school board.

8 The night men terrorise a local family, burning one of the men to death and badly scarring two others. Following this the Logan family keep guard during the dark, but the night men frighten the children when they visit the house late one night, even though they go away without taking any action.

0 The Logans refuse to shop at the local store, knowing that it is run by whites who are members of the night men. Papa and Mr Morrison are ambushed one night and Papa is injured and cannot return to work on the railroad. The local landowner is suspected of being behind the attack.

9 Cassie suffers humiliation when she is made to apologise for accidentally bumping into Lillian Jean Simms on the street, but later gains her revenge.T.J. finds himself ignored by the other students because of his unpleasant ways, and he takes to associating with white boys, thinking they are his friends.

Big Ma

Big Ma and Mrs Logan represent the changing face of the black world through the recent decades. Big Ma is a strong woman in her sixties and is grandmother to Cassie Logan. She is taller than her daughter-in-law, Mary Logan, and bigger. Her full name is Caroline Logan, but she is usually referred to as Big Ma. In Big Ma's early life it is doubtful that there would have been any opportunity to become a teacher, as her daughter-in-law has done. Her life has been one of hard physical labour, working in the fields with the men.

As the owner of the Logan land, Big Ma recognises that if she dies Harlan Granger might well attempt to challenge the right of her sons to inherit. Big Ma loves the land probably more than anyone else and she therefore shows a great deal of sense and foresight by arranging to sign papers which give the legal right to the land to her two remaining sons. She has been bothered for years by Harlan Granger, who wants to buy the land back, but her memories of the farm and the hard work which she has put into it mean that she will do as much as possible to prevent this from happening.

Big Ma has a close relationship with her daughter-in-law and grandchildren. Although she is able to use a gun and is prepared to do so to defend her home and family, Big Ma knows the dangers of behaviour that whites will see as provocative, which is why she is so concerned that Hammer might speak out or take action against Mr Simms or the Wallaces.

Ⓞ show support f love.

Mary Logan

Mary Logan is the mother of Cassie, Christopher-John, Little Man and Stacey. She is tawny coloured, thin and sinewy with <u>delicate features</u> in a <u>strong-jawed face</u> and is described as being <u>very pretty</u>. She is a <u>good teacher</u> and mother and represents a <u>newly emerging, independent-minded</u> class of blacks. The stand she takes over the matter of the 'new' books demonstrates her attitude to <u>racial equality</u> and her <u>personal integrity</u>. This is also visible when she refuses to alter what she was going to teach when the school board arrive to inspect her, and she has no hesitation in telling Harlan Grander that she <u>will not teach</u> what is in the books <u>about slavery</u> because it is <u>not true</u>. Her action in pasteing over the offensive list of names shocks the other teachers. She knows that her behaviour <u>threatens her teaching job</u> and that this is important for paying the family's bills, but does not allow this to sway her.

Mary is an <u>understanding and loving mother</u>, but she is also <u>very fair</u>. She almost certainly <u>understands Stacey's innocence</u> over the matter of cheating, but is driven to punish him when he will not accuse T.J. In the same way she agrees that Miss Crocker had <u>no alternative</u> but to whip Cassie and Little Man. She explains to Cassie why Big Ma had <u>no choice</u> but to make her apologise to Little Jean in Strawberry.

Mary's relationship with David, her husband, is one of <u>love, mutual trust and support</u>; they are <u>equal partners</u> in bringing up their family and striving to retain their land. She is grateful for Mr Morrison's presence but is anxious that he, like Uncle Hammer, should do nothing to put themselves at risk.

David Logan

David Logan is the children's father. Usually they refer to him as Papa. He is 6' 2'' tall and the youngest of a family of brothers, two of whom are now dead. There is a striking contrast in character between David and his remaining brother, Hammer. David is tied to the land. His whole life is devoted to ensuring that the family retains its hard-won heritage. He wants his children to inherit what he and his forebears have worked so hard to gain. He is a loving and caring father who is also very strict, as we witness when he punishes the children for their visit to the Wallaces' store. The children always know where they stand with their father and always know that he will treat their concerns seriously. He gives his children advice and helps them to see the importance of making their own decisions and taking the consequences for them, as when he advises Cassie to carefully consider whether seeking revenge on 'Miz' Lillian Jean is worth the risks involved in standing up for a principle.

David's attitude towards white people is obviously influenced by his own experiences. He shows himself to be a very determined and single-minded man when it comes to keeping hold of the land. Only when his family are at risk does this take second place. In setting fire to the fence he sacrifices a quarter of his cotton crop, but at the same time manages to stop the lynching of T.J. and the imminent attack on his own family.

Cassie

The story is told to us by Cassie Logan, who is nine years old when it begins. Because she is the narrator (story-teller) we do not get an outside view of her character and we therefore have to find out most of what we learn about her for ourselves. But Cassie also has a typical nine-year-old's honesty and her straightforward comments about other characters are often very revealing. Her direct and simple questions about things and her resentment at the racial intolerance she sees around her are made sharper for us because they come from a child.

Cassie is a bright, kind and caring person who has an independent mind. She has a strong sense of justice and a quick temper which, together with her courageous approach to unfairness, get her into trouble on a number of occasions. She refuses to accept a book at school when it becomes clear that it has been discarded by white students as being thought fit only for black children. She also shows enthusiasm for revenge: against whites who have wronged black families; against T.J. for cheating Stacey out of his new coat and losing her mother her teaching job; and after her father is attacked and hurt. Nevertheless, encouraged by her father, she learns that in her own best interests, and that of others, it is often wiser to react to events in a more thoughtful, planned and careful way.

Cassie's strong sense of justice sometimes causes her pain and suffering, as when Mr Barnett treats her differently to the white customers in his store. She cannot understand why he or Mr Simms treats her differently and it is only through such painful first-hand experiences that she learns about racism and intolerance. She feels betrayed and hurt when Big Ma fails to support her and it is only after her mother has explained the situation that Cassie is able to forgive her grandmother.

By the end of the story Cassie and the reader have learned a lot about what it meant to grow up as a black child in the <u>prejudiced</u> <u>and</u> <u>intolerant</u> <u>environment</u> of Mississippi in the 1930s.

Stacey

Stacey, at 12 years of age, is the eldest of the Logan children and, especially as his father is away for so much of the year, feels at times a particularly <u>sharp</u> <u>sense</u> <u>of</u> <u>responsibility</u>. We see this, for example, when he <u>worries</u> that the visit of the night men to the house and the threats of violence against the family are because of the wrecking of the school bus, which was <u>his</u> <u>idea</u>. Unlike his younger sister, Cassie, he has a <u>clear</u> <u>idea</u> about how things work in the <u>prejudiced</u> <u>and</u> <u>intolerant</u> times in which they live. In his careful planning to wreck the school bus he understands the importance of trying to make it look like an accident and of why the children should behave in a way that will not draw suspicion to them. He also knows that protesting against injustice has to be done with care, and therefore sees why Big Ma has to make Cassie apologise to 'Miz' Lillian Jean, even though it is Cassie who is in the right.

Stacey's friendship with T.J. never really recovers from T.J.'s <u>irresponsible</u> and <u>unkind</u> <u>treatment</u> <u>towards</u> <u>others</u>, and weakens further after T.J. tricks him into parting with his new coat. His <u>high</u> <u>standards</u> <u>of</u> <u>honour</u>, however, will not allow him to reveal that it is actually T.J. who has been guilty of cheating at school, or to say anything which would get others into trouble following their fight. T.J.'s betrayal of the children's mother finally convinces Stacey that he must look elsewhere for his friends. Nonetheless, towards the end of the novel Stacey feels <u>obliged</u> <u>to</u> <u>help</u> the injured T.J. home late at night after he has been beaten, although he is careful to make sure that none of the family are discovered there when the night men arrive. Stacey's behaviour during this incident shows calmness and maturity and he ensures that a warning of what is happening gets to his father in good time.

T.J. Avery

T.J. is a tall, thin boy who is feared by his own younger brother, Claude, and disliked by the other children in the story. He is a liar, a cheat, and a thief and although he uses his friendship with the Logan children to his own advantage, it is to them that he turns when he is in desperate need for help at the end of the novel. He is poorly disciplined at home – probably because his father is too ill to punish him – and has a weak character, which makes him easy prey for temptation. He is gullible and his need for attention results in him being easily tricked by the white Simms brothers into thinking that they are his friends, when in fact they regard him as a figure of fun to be used for their own amusement. T.J. is a strong contrast to the Logan children and his insecurity is the cause of much of his poor behaviour.

Uncle Hammer

Uncle Hammer lives in the North where, in theory, blacks are equal to whites and have the same rights. Understandably, therefore, Hammer finds the situation in the South very frustrating and his well-known fiery temper leads the rest of the family to worry about how he will react to events on a number of occasions. Hammer is generous towards the children, but has no sympathy when Stacey allows himself to be swindled out of the new coat which Hammer gives him.

Hammer takes pleasure in reminding the local whites that he considers himself their equal, both by the way he speaks to them and by the way he dresses and behaves. His purchase of a Packard car – identical to (but newer than) Harlan Granger's – is a deliberate act of defiance. His defiance also shows in his desire to seek immediate and violent revenge on local white racists who are known to have killed, hurt or victimised blacks. However, each time he is persuaded that this would be dangerous, or he restrains himself from doing anything which might endanger those he cares for.

Mr Morrison

Mr L.T. Morrison is an exceptionally tall and well-muscled man who has scars round his face and neck, as if caused by fire. At their first meeting with him, the children regard him as a 'giant'. He is brought home by David Logan (Papa) to look after the family while he is away working, but Mr Morrison soon becomes a valued member of the family. He acts as the family's guardian angel, guiding Stacey into the correct behaviour after the fight and earning his respect by saying that he will not tell his mother about it because he knows that Stacey will decide to tell her himself.

Although he is a man of great physical strength, Mr Morrison knows that the battle against inequality and prejudice cannot be won by brute force alone. Mr Morrison is a source of foresight, good judgement and integrity in the novel, as shown when he prevents the hot-headed Hammer from attacking Charlie Simms.

Harlan Granger

Harlan Granger lives very much according to the values of the past and despises all blacks. He sees it as his personal crusade to buy back all the land which used to belong to his family before the Civil War and he resents the Logans because they are independent people who will not sell. Harlan Granger typifies the racist bigot. His racist attitude is shown when he visits the Logans and tries to persuade them to sell their land. When they refuse he at once resorts to threats.

He resents and reacts violently to any suggestion that blacks could in any way be the equal of whites. It is clear that he is behind the sacking of Mary Logan and the bank manager's sudden calling in of their loan on the land. He is a man who holds a grudge for a long time; he still resents Mr Jamison because he sold some land to the Logans.

Wade Jamison

Mr Jamison is a white lawyer who recognises the injustices of the racial prejudice in the area. He does what he can to help blacks, and represents the changing attitudes of whites and the hope for a more tolerant society in the future. He willingly gives genuine advice, and he takes a very dangerous step when he agrees to guarantee their debts, especially as it seems likely that he may lose a lot of money as a result. He is well-mannered, calm and has a mask-like face which gives away very little of what he is thinking. Mr Jamison's actions at the end of the story prevent the certain hanging of T.J. by the mob. He ignores the threats made to his life, and the way many local whites regard him as a 'nigger lover', and tells the Logans that there are many whites who think as he does but who are as yet too afraid to speak out for fairness and justice.

Christopher-John

Christopher-John is a naturally cheerful and happy seven-year-old child. He is short and 'round', and likes it when everyone is at ease with everyone else. He dislikes arguments and his sensitivity to the atmosphere between people makes him unhappy when arguments erupt. His nature is naturally sunny and we learn early on that he 'took little interest in troublesome things, preferring to remain on good terms with everyone'.

Little Man

Little Man (Clayton Chester Logan) is a six-year-old who likes to keep himself spotlessly clean and neat. He is in the first grade at school as the story begins and is the one who is most hurt by the way the white children constantly torment and belittle blacks. He has a powerful sense of self-respect and shares the Logan family passion for justice and fairness. This is why he is reduced to tears when his clothes are dirtied once too often by the school bus and he complains bitterly to Big Ma. It also explains his strong reaction to the book he is given at school and the reason why he is prepared to be punished for refusing to take it rather than abandon his standards.

Jeremy Simms

Jeremy Simms is a white boy who accompanies the other children to and from the crossroads on their walk to school each day, for which he is often ridiculed by the other white children at his school. Although he is laughed at by many of the other white children, Jeremy perhaps represents the hope for the future in being the only white child to treat the Logans as friends and equals.

Lillian Jean Simms

Lillian Jean Simms is accidentally bumped by Cassie in the street in Strawberry and demands an apology. Although Cassie apologises, Lillian Jean is determined to <u>humiliate</u> her and is supported in this by her aggressive father. After humiliating Cassie, she fails completely to appreciate that Cassie's sudden friendship towards her is a ploy to get even. Eventually, after being beaten by Cassie in the forest, she becomes a little more <u>subdued</u> but still does not understand how <u>offensive</u> her behaviour has been or why Cassie has suddenly changed.

Melvin and R.W. Simms

Melvin and R.W. Simms are the two idle brothers who have <u>dropped</u> <u>out</u> of school and spend their time hanging around the stores and getting into trouble. They befriend T.J. and use him for amusement by <u>pretending</u> to be his friends. R.W. is especially vicious, as when he hits Mr Wallace and his wife in the robbery of their store.

Mildred Taylor

Mildred Delois Taylor was born in Jackson, Mississippi in 1943. Her family had lived in Mississippi since the days of slavery, but only three weeks after Taylor's birth the family moved north to Toledo, Ohio as her father did not want his daughter to grow up in the segregated, racist-ridden Southern states. Although Mildred Taylor lived in Ohio until graduating from the University of Toledo in 1965, the family frequently visited family members who continued to live in the South. It was during these visits that Taylor heard many stories, which were often concerned with the values of courage, dignity and self-respect. Through these stories Taylor came to recognise the difference between the view of life they presented of black people in America and that presented in the 'official' history books of the time.

Later, Mildred Taylor recalled how she was entranced as a child, listening to the relatives and neighbours tell stories about the past. This oral tradition of story-telling runs through *Roll of Thunder*, not just in the way Big Ma or Mr Morrison recall their ancestors and the heritage of the past to Cassie and the other children, but also in the general structure of the novel, with its emphasis on recounting events through the eyes of Cassie as a narrator and on keeping them strictly in chronological order.

After graduating from the University of Toledo, Taylor joined the Peace Corps and went to teach in Ethiopia and her experiences there caused her to remember the stories about the strength, pride and dignity of her own relatives told by her father and other family members.

When she returned to the United States in 1967, she continued to work for the Peace Corps and, in 1968, she achieved a Master's degree from the University of Colorado. During this period the Black Power movements was at its height and Taylor joined the Black Student Alliance and played a part in the establishment of a Black Studies programme at Colorado university. Taylor's studies extended into all areas of black culture, history and politics.

After moving to Los Angeles, she began to focus on her writing and, after several years, she achieved her first success when she won a competition sponsored by the Council of Interracial Books for children. Her winning story, *Song of the Trees*, was based on an old Logan family story told through the eyes of the eight-year-old Cassie. This was the first of Taylor's 'Logan family' books. *The Well*: *David's Story* (1995), which tells the story of the ten-year-old David Logan, Cassie's father, is the last. A related book, *Mississippi Bridge* (1990), is narrated not by Cassie but by Jeremy Simms, who appears in *Roll of Thunder, Hear My Cry*. She also explores the theme of racism in two other books, *The Friendship* (1987) and *The Gold Cadillac* (1987).

Taylor now lives in Colorado and has received a number of awards and honours for her work.

Segregation was common in 1930s southern America.

Between the sixteenth and nineteenth centuries, millions of men, women and children were transported by ship from West Africa, where they were exchanged for goods, to America. In the ships they were tightly packed together under inhuman conditions and many died on the journey. On arrival in America the survivors were used as slaves, mostly in the Southern states. Most slaves then worked under cruel and hard conditions in the cotton, sugar or tobacco plantations from dawn until dusk – even the children, if they were over five years old. The plantations were owned by whites who, as their owners, had complete control over the lives of the slaves and could mistreat them, or buy and sell them, as they saw fit.

When Abraham Lincoln became President of The Union in 1861 he was not well liked in the South because of his very outspoken condemnation of slavery, and when it was banned seven states broke away from The Union and called themselves The Confederate States of America. When Lincoln called out the troops after the Confederates attacked a government fort, four more states broke away and the four-year-long Civil War began between the North (Yankees) and the South (Confederates). After huge casualties on both sides, the North (Yankees) won. Even so, newly emancipated (freed) slaves were not always accepted even in the North, and Lincoln's reforms were not popular everywhere. Even in the 1930s, when *Roll of Thunder, Hear My*

Cry is set, many white Southern landowners still clung to these old values and were extremely resentful or antagonistic towards any blacks who tried to better themselves or make their own way in life. These whites often saw such aspirations as the blacks (or 'niggers' as they insultingly called them) getting 'above themselves' or 'getting uppity'.

Roll of Thunder, Hear My Cry focuses on the experiences of black people living in the South during a period when America experienced severe economic depression resulting in widespread unemployment and poverty for many people, both black and white. The white landlords made sure that black people were kept 'in their place', and the vast majority lived on land that was owned by a landlord. Very few black people owned their own land and often, when they did, it caused the kind of resentment among white people that Taylor describes in *Roll of Thunder, Hear My Cry*.

Segregation was the norm at this time (it continued until very recent times), and black children attended all-black schools while the white children went to far better equipped white schools. Black people were often refused service in restaurants or had to sit in a special area, had to use special toilets and washrooms and were sometimes not allowed on buses. The whites did not want the blacks to own property and there was no justice for them under a legal system run by whites. White people could more or less treat black people as they liked. This kind of injustice continued long after the 1930s described in Taylor's book and was still commonplace in many Southern areas well into the 1960s.

Some white people did not agree with such racist attitudes, but if they tried to do something about it they too were likely to suffer intimidation or violence from racist white people. The Ku Klux Klan, a kind of racist secret society like the 'night men', that terrorised black people, particularly those who stood up for their rights or tried to better themselves, was particularly active at this time. They carried out all kinds of atrocities on black people – lynchings were not uncommon, nor were beatings or burning the property of black people.

Themes and images

Land ownership

Land and its ownership underlies much of what happens in the story. The history of black people in America dates from when they were taken from their own lands in Africa and sold into slavery. Even in the period after slavery was abolished, black people were essentially dispossessed. Therefore, to own land in the 1930s signified more than possession. It meant independence and freedom. With the freeing of the slaves and the granting of the right to own property, it became possible for blacks to own land. The Logans own 200 acres of land outright and another 200 acres for which they have a mortgage. The importance to them, psychologically and financially, of owning their own land is stressed in almost every chapter of the novel and their struggle to retain it governs much of their working lives and often directly affects their behaviour.

Black people owning land in Mississippi is seen as provocative by most local whites. It increases the racists' hatred and provides them with the motivation for physical violence.

Big Ma takes Harlan Granger's threats to get the land back very seriously and she therefore arranges to transfer the ownership of her land to her two sons. Hammer is prepared to sacrifice all he owns to keep the land safe – even his beautiful car. Even though he is extremely proud of it, he takes the very down-to-earth view that a car cannot grow crops or become a home in which to raise a family.

David works away from home on the railway in order to increase the family's earnings. He teaches his children about the value of the land so that they will one day understand its importance. For the Logans, retaining the land is central to their lives. Their energies are directed towards ensuring they have the money to pay the mortgage. At first, Cassie cannot understand why the land is so important to the family, but by the end of the story this has changed and when she cries for T.J. and the land, she is also crying for freedom, dignity and equality.

Racial prejudice

Cassie learns, as does Stacey, that friendships between blacks and whites are not permitted and that whites have to be addressed by their full names – even the children have to be spoken to using titles like 'Miz', normally reserved for adults. Whites, on the other hand, speak to blacks in offensive terms, calling them 'boy', or 'nigger', freely. Blacks are expected to accept inferior treatment in shops, at the market and even when walking down the street. Even so, people like Harlan Granger and the Wallaces bitterly resent any small freedoms allowed to black people. In all their actions they show bitterness, whether by charging for goods not supplied, scheming to take land that is not theirs, or setting people on fire. For black people there is no recourse to justice for these events. To publicly complain would bring more violence and persecution on their heads, as Cassie learns in Strawberry when she dares to remind Mr Barnett that he has kept Cassie and Stacey waiting while he served white people before them.

Plantation owners pay their sharecroppers very little and even then they arrange matters so that they take most of what the sharecroppers grow and overcharge them for credit at the only stores they are allowed to use. Again, there is nothing the blacks can do about this.

Even the local sheriff calls a black woman witness a liar and makes no effort to see that T.J. gets proper treatment instead of being threatened with hanging by a mob, or that the whites who beat or kill blacks are brought to book.

In spite of this Stacey successfully takes revenge on the Jefferson Davis school bus, Cassie humiliates Lillian Jean, and the Logans manage to keep their land.

Justice

Cassie begins to understand that there is little justice for black people. Their school and its facilities are vastly inferior to those at Jefferson Davis school (where white children go), as can be seen by the black children having to use very old, dog-eared textbooks that have been thrown out by the white school. Even here the authorities make it look as though they are doing the black students a favour by donating the books to them. The white children have a bus to take them to school, whereas the black children have a long and tiring walk. As if this were not enough, the white children's bus daily threatens the black children's lives for the amusement of its occupants, often causing the black children to dive into the ditch to avoid it or to be soaked as the driver deliberately drives through puddles to drench them. Even the school terms are shorter in the black school because it is recognised that the black children will be working the land during the spring and summer months. The black schoolteachers' pay is low and the working conditions inferior.

History of slavery

The historical background against which the events are set is very important, and the struggle against the history of slavery and the presence of racial prejudice and intolerance is central to the story. This is true both for the blacks and also for some of the whites. The history of the slave trade and its evil practices, such as the breeding farms, is explained to the children and Mr Morrison's childhood serves as a powerful example of this. The behaviour of black families in the novel is set in this context and influenced by the way they are treated by society. Through Big Ma and Mr Morrison, we learn how important it is for the black families to know about their history, to help them to come to terms with the present.

Growing up

The story is related in chronological order and tells of about ten months in the life of the children, starting from October 1933. During this brief period the children grow up considerably as a result of what happens around them and to them and learn important lessons about life.

Stacey has to come to terms with the actions of his friend, T.J., the 'intrusion' of Mr Morrison into the household, the brutal assault on his father, and the savage attack on T.J. His action in destroying the school bus, while successful, is dangerous. His pursuit of T.J. to the Wallaces is unwise, but understandable. When he gives his coat away he is responding to wounded vanity. Later, however, he shows greater maturity when he refuses to be fooled into giving T.J. the whistle from Jeremy. His punishment of T.J. after his mother loses her job is both calculating and effective. But despite everything, Stacey is still able to cry for his friend when it becomes obvious that T.J. has a very poor hold on life.

Cassie is more bewildered by the world she finds herself in; she cannot understand the injustices around her and does not recognise their dangers. She stands up against her teacher in support of Little Man but does not realise the danger of behaving like this when white people are involved. She comes close to disaster when she confronts the shopkeeper at Barnett's Mercantile, and immediately afterwards she falls foul of Mr Simms when she attempts to argue her rights. This is a low point for Cassie, but her revenge upon Lillian Jean is well-planned and executed. She shows a great deal of sensitivity, particularly in her response to the loneliness of Jeremy, for her mother after the dismissal from her job, and for T.J. when she cries for him at the end of the book.

Text commentary

Chapters 1–3

Chapter 1

> ❝*I tugged again at my collar and dragged my feet*❞

We learn a lot about each of the children in the first few pages of the novel. Taylor skilfully mixes <u>speech</u> with Cassie's <u>private</u> <u>thoughts</u>. Cassie feels imprisoned by her clothes and it is clear that she normally does not wear shoes. She feels the restriction of attending school all the more when she thinks of all the other things she could be doing instead. Little Man is delighted with his <u>neat</u> <u>and</u> <u>clean</u> appearance. Stacey appears <u>subdued</u>, in contrast to Christopher-John, who is characteristically <u>cheerful</u>. Notice how this device allows you to quickly get to know something of the children, their standard of living, their <u>relationships</u> with each other and about their mother's teaching job at the school. It also allows Cassie to 'drift off' into her own thoughts, which – as she is the <u>narrator</u> of the story – we then 'overhear' and learn about the history of how the Logans got their land.

Explore

Think about your initial impressions of each of the characters and write down your ideas.

> ❝'*Ah, man, don't look so down,*' *T.J. said cheerfully.*❞

Stacey is subdued at the thought of spending all year being taught by his mother. When T.J. praises her teaching we see the author's <u>ironic</u> <u>humour</u>; Cassie observes to herself that her mother had been so successful with T.J. last year that he was 'returning for a second try'. We see this same humorous touch a little later on, where it is also used to emphasise how young Little Man is when he innocently asks T.J. what death looks like, completely ruining the atmosphere of suspense which T.J. was trying to build up.

The prospect of Stacey being in his mother's class immediately suggests for T.J. the possibility of passing his examinations by <u>cheating</u>. This dishonest and 'street-wise' attitude is an important feature of T.J.'s character which is cleverly introduced here the first time we meet him.

> ❝ *Burning? What burning?* ❞

We see that T.J. likes to be <u>involved</u> in matters which are probably too old for him. Cassie has already told her mother about T.J.'s visits to a <u>disreputable</u> local store, for which he has got his own brother Claude into trouble rather than <u>take the blame himself</u>.

Explore

Look at the way our negative view of T.J. is cleverly and quickly generated by what he says, his attitude to others and the kinds of values he has, together with the Logan children's reactions towards him.

Taylor is careful not to produce stereotypical characters, and we see in the story <u>admirable</u> and <u>flawed</u> individuals, <u>both black and white</u>. T.J. is 'balanced', in this respect, by Jeremy Simms, just as Harlan Granger is balanced by Mr Jamison. Other balances also appear and you should be on the lookout for them in this carefully crafted novel.

> ❝ *spewing clouds of red dust like a huge yellow dragon breathing fire* ❞

The bus is an uncontrollable, fierce monster from which there is <u>little chance</u> to escape and is a <u>symbol</u> of the <u>cruel</u> and <u>racist</u> way many local whites behave towards blacks. More evidence of this appears in Chapter 3, when the behaviour of the bus and the way it is described as 'a living thing, plaguing and defeating us at every turn' emphasise it as a symbol for the real enemy in their lives.

> ❝*There was an awkward silence.*❞

Explore

Do you think the bus driver is deliberately trying to hit the children? Would he or his employers be upset, do you suppose, if one of them was killed 'accidentally'?

Jeremy Simms is a young white boy who, unlike many adults, is happy to offer <u>friendship</u> for its own sake, irrespective of the colour of the skin of others. His friendship is not always well-received by the Logan children, or by his own family and other white children. Jeremy's behaviour emphasises that there is <u>hope</u> for the future between black and white, and that this hope lies in the children. David Logan – the children's father – offers Stacey advice about this later, in Chapter 7.

> ❝*four weather-beaten wooden houses on stilts of brick*❞

The description of the school and its setting tells us much about the life of the black community. It is <u>deprived</u> and tumble-down and in many senses has its 'back to the wall'. Even the amount of education which black children get is less than whites, and the drop-out rate is very high.

Explore

Notice that after the first day many of the clothes which the children wear will be put away. Why is this?

The name of Great Faith School is significant, as is its location next to the community church. This represents the <u>hope</u> <u>for</u> <u>the</u> <u>future</u> for black families. Everything about the school is in contrast to the <u>luxuriously</u> equipped Jefferson Davis School for whites, with its flag of Mississippi, emblazoned with the Confederate emblem, deliberately flying above the American flag in the centre of its expansive front lawn.

> **_Girls with blond braids and boys with blue eyes stared up at me._**

The news that the class are going to have books is met with <u>enthusiasm</u> and Little Man's 'face lit in eager excitement'. However, when he sees that they are the dirty and worn-out cast offs of the white school he <u>rejects</u> his copy. Notice that once Little Man has taken a stand Cassie sides with him. This is not simply loyalty to her brother – as she tries to explain to Miss Crocker. But like many other adults, both black and white, Miss Crocker looked at life around her but 'understood nothing' of what it meant.

Explore

Why is Cassie's first view of inside her book so revealing for us? Why is her younger brother's reaction so much more extreme?

> **_Biting the hand that feeds you. That's what you're doing, Mary Logan ..._**

Mary Logan <u>understands</u> why the books have caused a problem and, although she is careful not to <u>undermine the</u> <u>authority</u> of Daisy Crocker, she makes it clear that she has no intention of encouraging her children to accept the <u>unfairness</u> of the world the way it is. Like her children, Mary Logan <u>refuses</u> to be defined by what others think, and this is why she covers the offensive pages in the books. For the same reason, she later refuses to abide by what the textbooks say about the history of slavery when she knows it to be a <u>distortion</u>, even though her stand on this issue costs her dearly.

Cassie overhears the conversation between her mother and Miss Crocker. This <u>device</u> is used several times in the book to allow us to 'overhear' things which we are not told directly. This <u>technique</u> cleverly draws the reader into the story by allowing them to 'know' things which some of the characters do not.

Mama's origins outside the county make her something of an 'outsider', even after 14 years. This tells us a lot about how the more traditional thinkers like Miss Crocker regard anything which disturbs their lives. It also helps to explain why entrenched attitudes are so hard to change in such communities, even today.

Chapter 2

> ❝Papa, what you doing home?❞

Explore

What hints are we given in this chapter that Papa may have returned home because all is not well?

Welcome though their father's return is, it is clear that he is not expected. While Chapter 1 concentrated on the children's view of their lives, Chapter 2 tells us something about how the adults in the Logan family see the world around them.

> ❝the most formidable-looking being we had ever encountered❞

Notice the way in which Mr Morrison is described – he is a 'tree', towering over their father's six feet two inches, with a 'massive body', skin scarred 'as if by fire', with deep lifelines in his face and 'clear and penetrating' eyes. His stature is that of some god-like 'giant' whose voice is 'like the roll of low thunder'. His attributes make him immune to the physical threats by which the local whites terrorise the black community. The most significant thing the children learn from him is that in spite of his immensely powerful presence, he is a softly-spoken, peaceable man who avoids physical violence wherever possible. It is clear that he was blamed for the fight which got him sacked from his job because he was black, not because he was in the wrong.

"Its walls were made of smooth oak"

The Logan house has a strong sense of <u>family</u> <u>history</u>, of the family's <u>traditions</u> and its ancestors, and has a feeling of permanence and continuity. It is a stable, established, solid home. Notice the number of items which are of oak or walnut – which are slow-growing and long-lived trees. The living strength and permanence of timber and trees (like those planted by Big Ma and Grandpa Logan) are a symbol of the <u>strength</u> which the black community draws from its history, tradition and inheritance, and the 'roots' which have been put down in their land.

'Sayin' they'd do it again if some uppity nigger get out of line.'

Explore

If some whites feel so secure about their behaviour that they can brag publicly that they will do the same again, why is it that they need the pretence of some excuse?

The whites in the story always like to have some <u>excuse</u> – however flimsy – for their <u>persecution</u> of blacks. Mr Morrison was accused of starting the fight and was sacked. What was John Henry Berry supposed to have done? You are given considerable cause to suppose that he was in fact <u>innocent</u> of doing anything wrong. It is clear that <u>some whites</u> regularly go around terrorising and killing blacks and that very little is done about this by the rest of the white community, as their actions are well known by everyone.

"In this family, we don't shop at the Wallace store."

At first sight, Papa's statement seems strange and meaningless. What is it that tells us that he has touched on a dangerous topic? (Look at the reactions of the other adults). Papa gives the children a <u>reason</u> for avoiding the Wallace store but later, in Chapter 4,

Explore

Would the children be more frightened if their parents told them all their worries? Is this something which modern parents also do with their children?

we learn that there is <u>more</u> <u>to</u> <u>it</u> than this. Like their mother, Papa tells the children enough to keep them safe and out of trouble, and advises them about their behaviour, but <u>does</u> <u>not</u> <u>reveal</u> all his <u>worries</u> and <u>thoughts</u>. We are aware of this on a number of occasions when the adults in the family talk but the children are sent to bed. Occasionally the children overhear snippets of conversation which frightens them.

Chapter 3

> ❝*Nigger! Nigger! Mud eater!* ❞

The children's carefully calculated revenge against the bus contains a lesson about how blacks must deal with white persecution. Stacey knows that it is important to be sure that they are <u>not</u> <u>suspected</u> and that the crash be made to look like an accident. He knows that none of them must speak of the plan either before or afterwards and, significantly, he excludes the <u>loud-mouthed</u> T.J. from everything to do with the incident. He will not even tell his own brothers and sister what his plan is beforehand. Later on we see Cassie successfully adopt the <u>same</u> <u>approach</u> to dealing with 'Miz' Lillian Jean. Papa also follows this method when dealing with the mob by setting the fire at the end of the novel. <u>Contrast</u> this with the <u>bragging</u> <u>behaviour</u> of the whites who persecute local families. Dealing successfully with bullying and intolerance is a matter of <u>actions</u> <u>speaking</u> <u>louder</u> <u>than</u> <u>words</u>, and by the end of the novel Cassie has <u>learnt</u> that there are some things, like the burning of the cotton, which are never to be spoken of, not even within the family, and that the sweetest revenge is the most well concealed.

> **"Jeremy never rode the bus, no matter how bad the weather."**

Every time Jeremy tries to make friends with the children he is <u>rebuffed</u> or, as here, <u>rejected</u> <u>outright</u>. It is not easy to answer the question of why Jeremy persists in offering his friendship to Stacey and his family, given the sort of background and family Jeremy comes from. <u>Compare</u> Jeremy's behaviour with that of Mr Jamison for a possible explanation for the way he treats the Logans. Both are examples of <u>admirable</u> white characters who are <u>abused</u> by other whites for daring to step outside accepted patterns of <u>bigoted</u> <u>behaviour</u>.

Notice how, in keeping with the way it has been described so far, the destruction of the bus appears as the death of some living creature which 'sputtered a last murmuring protest' before dying 'like a lopsided billy goat on its knees'. Notice also that although the bus is thoroughly wrecked, the children have gained victory without hurting anyone.

Explore

Why do you think Jeremy keeps trying to be friendly and why does he never go on the bus? Why does he want to be friends with Stacey when he could presumably have plenty of white friends?

> **"Then all of us began to laugh"**

We are not told whether the rest of the family know the <u>truth</u> about the crashing of the bus, but the incident causes much <u>amusement</u> in the Logan household and we may wonder how much they suspect. This is a nice touch by Taylor, who seems to have left us to wonder for ourselves how much is known but <u>unspoken</u> – especially as the adults never question the children in any depth about their persistent amusement following the crash.

> ❝It don't take but a little of nothin' to set them devilish night men off.❞

As soon as Mama suspects what Mr Avery has called about she packs the children off to bed, but they sneak back to overhear him say that the night men ride whenever they feel that the blacks are stepping out of their place. Notice how the mention of Mr Grimes, the appropriately named school bus driver, causes Stacey to assume that it is the wrecking of the bus which has prompted events. Notice too how his <u>guilt</u> about this causes him to snap at the others, although his <u>growing sense of adult responsibility</u> also causes him to offer to help deal with the threat. Later, we learn from T.J. that Stacey appears to have worried for nothing, although given T.J.'s unreliability we are never fully sure about the truth. There are several places in the novel where this device is used to leave the reader in <u>suspense</u> about what is really happening. This technique contrasts cleverly with the way the story is recounted via Cassie to lead us to think we are being told everything.

> ❝a shadowy figure outlined by the headlights of the car behind him stepped out.❞

Taylor's skill in controlling <u>tension</u> is also evident when, later that night, Cassie wakens to find that Big Ma and her rifle have gone. Hearing a noise on the porch and assuming it to be her brothers, she goes out and is terrified when the dog leaps on her, affectionately licking her face. Swiftly following her relief comes terror as she sees the night men approaching. Notice how their presence is more terrifying because they do not actually do anything – it is the <u>threat</u> of what they might have done which is so frightening. The sight of the protective Mr Morrison hiding in the darkness further heightens the tension, producing uncontrollable trembling in Cassie.

Uncover the plot

Delete two of the three alternatives given, to find the correct plot.

1   Cassie Logan and her cousins/brothers/neighbours Little Man, Stacey and Christopher-John live in Alabama/Louisiana/Mississippi with their mother and their housekeeper/grandmother/cook, Big Ma.

2   A teacher, Miss Lanier/Davis/Crocker, gives out some books. Berry/Little Man/T.J. and Cassie/Mary Lou/Gracey are beaten when they refuse to accept them because they have been bought/used/discarded by white children.

3   One winter's day on the way to school the children are forced into the slimy gully/wet forest/schoolyard by the passing school bus. Stacey/Little Man/Cassie plans revenge.

4   The children secretly bury a log/dig a hole/pile up rocks in the road. The bus driver does not sense the danger and the bus crashes/stops/is covered in mud.

Who? What? Why? When? Where?

1   Why, in the Spring of 1931, did Papa set out looking for work on the railroad?

2   Why do Cassie, Little Man and Stacey dislike T.J.?

3   What does Papa mean when he threatens the children that he will 'wear y'all out'?

4   Where did 'the burning' take place?

5   Why is Stacey especially upset at the news about the night men?

Character clues

1   Who is more afraid of T.J. than of their own mother?

2   Who does Miss Crocker think is 'Biting the hand that feeds you'?

3   Who refused to pick up a book?

4   Who has 'a deep, quiet voice like the low roll of thunder'?

5   Whose body is racked with uncontrollable trembling?

Chapters 4–6

Chapter 4

> **"** *Somethin' the matter with that child, Mary.* **"**

Explore

Why does Cassie not tell her mother what is worrying her? What else would she have to reveal?

The <u>technique</u> which we saw used at the end of the last chapter is here seen again, but <u>cleverly reversed</u>. Because we and the children overheard the adults' conversation, we know about the children's fear of the night men. But the adults do not know that the children <u>overheard</u>, so now we know something which the adults do not. Notice how this <u>conspiratorial</u> <u>tone</u> is maintained when Cassie overhears Big Ma and Mama discussing how worried they are about her.

Explore

Why do you suppose T.J. behaves in this foolish and immature way? Think of what he is always trying to get from the other children.

T.J. has a system for getting out of work. The 'system' he talks about is, typically for him, one which involves <u>dishonesty</u>. So we are not surprised when he adopts the same approach to passing his school tests. In telling what he knows about the night men, T.J. speaks the truth when he says that these are things which he should not know about. Look carefully at T.J.'s attitude when describing what happened to Mr Tatum – this tells us how far from being mature, sensitive and grown up T.J. is.

> **"** *…big test coming up* **"**

It seems possible that T.J. <u>stole</u> the test answers from Mama's room, as he has provided himself with a sheet of notes. In any event, Stacey's ripping them up does not stop T.J. making another set and, worse still, deliberately allowing Stacey to <u>take the blame</u> for him using them in the examination. In <u>contrast</u> to the way T.J. behaves, Stacey refuses to incriminate anyone else

and takes the full blame himself. This includes a public whipping from his own mother in front of the class. Stacey's mother is here in the <u>same</u> <u>position</u> as Big Ma later in the novel, when Cassie is bullied in Strawberry. Both these events, like those which ultimately befall T.J., show how it is sometimes the case that being in the right is less important than how things are made to <u>appear</u> to others.

Stacey's determination to punish T.J. is strong enough for him to <u>disobey</u> his father and follow T.J. to the Wallace store, where the Wallaces laugh at 'all the little niggers' who have come to dance. Notice how, even during the fight, T.J.'s <u>mean</u> <u>and</u> <u>underhand</u> attitude is shown – he can gain the advantage only by pretending to be more hurt than he is.

❝*Mr Morrison towered above us.*❞

Mr Morrison intervenes to stop the fight. Notice how, when he passes the Wallace brothers, he 'looked through them as though they were not there'. This is both a measure of his <u>attitude</u> towards them and a skilful indication of the <u>emptiness</u> and <u>worthlessness</u> of their characters – they are vacant, idle people of no substance.

Explore

How do you think T.J. would have dealt with the same situation? How does the immediate reaction of Stacey's mother – compared with what the children were expecting – tell you that she recognises this increased maturity in her son?

Stacey recognises that he owes it to his mother to tell her the <u>truth</u>. He becomes much closer to Mr Morrison after Mr Morrison makes it plain that he will not be reporting the matter of the fight to Mama, because Stacey himself will. As this is precisely the point Stacey was defending at school – that T.J. should have had the character to admit his own errors but that others should not do it for him – so we should not be surprised that Stacey does finally own up about the fight to his mother. Again, he does so without implicating anyone else.

" *he bought himself two hundred acres* **"**

Big Ma tells Cassie about the strong <u>sense</u> <u>of</u> <u>unity</u> which she feels exists between her and the land. Her history, her memories of loved ones, her past losses and her grief are all <u>evoked</u> <u>by</u> <u>the</u> <u>land</u>. This long section, carefully written as a conversation, is more of a look into Big Ma's history and her mind than a real chat between her and Cassie. It is also a very skilful way of telling the reader much of what they need to know to really understand the significance of many events in the story. We sense that Big Ma's <u>memories</u> draw her very strongly. She and the land are almost of one spirit, having grown old together through their various trials and tribulations. Significantly, the land means <u>almost</u> <u>nothing</u> in itself for Harlan Granger, who has more land already than he knows what to do with.

Telling Cassie about people and incidents from the past keeps them alive for Big Ma. The importance of this <u>tradition</u> of story-telling, and the way it preserves a <u>cultural</u> <u>history</u> for the black community as a whole, is an idea which runs through the novel.

" *the skin was scarred, burned, and the lips were wizened black* **"**

The children are shown first-hand what some whites are prepared to do to blacks, and understand how such enemies are <u>dangerous</u>. More than any whipping or scolding, this explains to the children why they should not visit the Wallace store.

Explore

Why, during their visit, do you think Mrs Berry is so cheerful?

The strength of the <u>rule</u> <u>of</u> <u>law</u> and <u>justice</u> is can be seen from the way the Wallaces openly laugh about disfiguring Mr Berry, and indicates how carefully blacks must behave to protect themselves from similar treatment.

> **"I don't want you to ever go to their store again."**

Following their visit to the Berrys, the children witness the character and courage of their mother as she tries to persuade other families not to shop at the Wallace store. The growing strength of the anger of local families is shown by the fact that even after what happened to Mr Berry, some families are prepared to consider siding with Mama. But notice that everyone is careful to avoid talking openly about the Wallaces' actions, because that is not wise – 'There were too many ears that listened for others besides themselves, and too many tongues that wagged to those they shouldn't.' (Which character does this remind you of?)

The importance of the Logans' land is again emphasised; it is this which means that they do not have to 'kowtow', or defer, to white landowners, unlike many other families.

Chapter 5

> **"Strawberry was nothing like the tough, sprawling bigness I had envisioned."**

The twenty-two miles to Strawberry is a long trip by wagon and although Stacey has been allowed to go before, it is clear that Cassie is being taken only because Big Ma has promised Mr Avery to take T.J., whom she obviously does not like very much. Cassie cannot see why Big Ma parks her wagon so far away from the best spot on the field. By now, you should be able to see why Big Ma's comment, 'Them's white folks' wagons', explains everything. In keeping with the way suspense is used to maintain interest throughout the novel, notice how the author

Explore

Following such strong warnings, why do things go so badly wrong for Cassie later that day?

does not tell the reader why Big Ma is visiting Wade Jamison. In fact the reader has to <u>work this out</u> alone (look at what happens in the second half of Chapter 7). Big Ma finds T.J.'s constant chattering tiresome, and later tells him to be quiet on the journey home. Cassie <u>suspects</u> that this is why she has been allowed along, but it is not T.J. whom Big Ma warns about not wanting any trouble.

> ❝ *The Barnett Mercantile had everything* ❞

Against his better judgement, Stacey leaves the wagon after being persuaded by T.J., followed by a reluctant Cassie. How likely is it that Cassie or Stacey would have left the wagon of their own accord? What sort of an influence on others is T.J.? Cassie is at a loss to understand why T.J. admires the gun so much – in her <u>innocence</u> she cannot fathom what use it would be. But Stacey backs away nervously, knowing that the store is a hostile place for them. What is it that T.J. thinks the gun will give him that he does not already have?

Cassie remarks that the gun would not even be good enough to 'hardly kill a rattlesnake'. Not for the first time, T.J. speaks truer than he perhaps knows when he answers that 'there's other things a body needs protectin' from more than a rattlesnake'. Although T.J. has in mind his own notion of what these 'other things' are, it seems clear that his thinking does not include the idea that people need 'protecting' in another sense – the <u>love and protection</u> of a <u>family</u> and <u>strong moral values</u> might, for example, have prevented T.J. ending up where he eventually does.

> ❝ *you ever seen a gun like that before in your whole life?* ❞

T.J.'s longing for <u>respect</u> and <u>attention</u> mistakenly leads him to imagine that these can be gained by owning a gun which is clearly

Explore

Which other characters is T.J., perhaps unconsciously, copying here? Who else has this kind of attitude to others?

designed not for hunting food, but for killing people. Read carefully the conversation between Cassie and her mother near the start of Chapter 6 for a clearer understanding of the important point being made here.

❝I ain't nobody's little nigger!❞

Cassie is <u>furious</u> at the way Mr Barnett is treating them. But the older Stacey and T.J. do not protest at all, because they have <u>learned</u> <u>something</u> that Cassie is only now <u>beginning</u> to fully realise. When she protests to Stacey that Mr Barnett was in the wrong, he replies, 'I know it and you know it, but he don't know it, and that's where the trouble is'. Which other young member of the Logan family have we seen already start to learn this painful lesson? Find the description of Cassie's behaviour when alone after leaving the store and notice how it emphasises her <u>youthful</u> <u>impetuosity</u>.

❝It was then that I bumped into Lillian Jean Simms.❞

Because she is still preoccupied with her recent run-in with Mr Barnett, Cassie does not see Lillian Jean and accidentally walks into her. Although she apologises, Lillian Jean demands a <u>humiliating</u> <u>apology</u> from Cassie by saying she should walk in the dirty road. For the second time that day Cassie is insulted, when Lillian Jean contrasts her 'nasty little self' with 'decent white folks'. The fact that Lillian Jean feels that she has some kind of <u>natural</u> <u>right</u> to treat Cassie this way tells us a lot about the upbringing of many white children and the <u>values</u> their parents taught them. Remember that in Chapter 1 Lillian Jean has already bragged that Jeremy's bruises were the result of his friendship with blacks.

Explore

Notice how Jeremy tries to defend Cassie both to his sister and his father. We can see why Mr Simms' behaviour would frighten Cassie, but why is Jeremy afraid?

Mr Simms, backed by his family and other townsfolk, bullies Cassie and Big Ma – who Mr Simms insultingly refers to as 'aunty' – into a humiliating apology. Only later does Cassie come to <u>understand</u> how little choice in the matter Big Ma had. Once she is away from her home, Big Ma knows how exposed she is. Like the incident in the Barnett store, Cassie is <u>angered</u> by the way she has been treated, but more by what she sees as betrayal and a deliberate lack of support from her own family. This is why the day has been 'cruel' to her.

Chapter 6

> **❝** *a tall, handsome man, nattily dressed in a gray pin-stripped suit* **❞**

Explore

What important contrast with the children's father is revealed by the way Taylor introduces us to Uncle Hammer? (Look especially at the description of his eyes.)

Stacey explains why Big Ma had <u>no real choice</u> in Strawberry, but is Cassie also right in saying that her father would not have made her apologise? Your conclusion will depend on your assessment of David Logan's character. For Cassie it is a matter of either being on her side of things or not, and we now meet Uncle Hammer, who is somewhat like-minded to Cassie.

What does Uncle Hammer's dress and the fact that he has bought a car like Harlan Granger's, say about his character (apart from that he has money)? Big Ma's reaction contains a clue here. Big Ma knows her son's character well, and tries several times to prevent him hearing about what has happened in Strawberry.

> **❝** *I ain't gotta use David's gun… I got my own.* **❞**

When Hammer hears about what happened in Strawberry, why does Mrs Logan immediately send Stacey for Mr Morrison? Which other character wants their own gun, and do these two

Text commentary

people have anything in common? Notice how Christopher-John adopts the same attitude towards <u>instant revenge</u> as Cassie and Uncle Hammer, but that other members of the family, notably Stacey, do not. What character trait does Mr Morrison have which will be essential in successfully dealing with this situation?

❝*that's the way of things Cassie*❞

Mrs Logan <u>explains</u> to Cassie why things are the way they are, and why Big Ma had little option in Strawberry but to behave the way she did. Her mother also explains something even more important in response to Cassie's 'White ain't nothin'!', and she <u>begins to learn</u> why it is that some people – both white and black – need to feel superior: because they have so little else. Mrs Logan's account of why Mr Simms thinks the way he does is central to the novel and you should study it carefully.

❝*Uncle Hammer's going to take us to church.*❞

The family's preparations for attending church are an example of Mrs Logan's comment to Cassie about the importance of people making the best of their lives. (Notice that the way Cassie regards her mother is subtly emphasised by the description of her hair before she shapes it.) Against this background of making do, Hammer gives Stacey a new wool coat as an advance Christmas present. Although Stacey feels <u>too grown up</u> now to give Hammers a hug, and shakes hands instead, the way he gives the coat away will show that he still has <u>a lot of maturing</u> to do yet.

Hammer's car and Stacey's new coat create a strong impression at church, although T.J.'s reaction to the coat is typically <u>envious</u>. Why does Stacey feel so hurt by T.J.'s comments? Cassie clearly wants to prevent T.J. getting a ride in Hammer's new car, as punishment for insulting Stacey and, probably, because the rest of the children do not like him. But why, when Mama suggests that T.J. might like a ride, does Cassie speak up 'before Stacey could reply', and what does it say about Stacey's <u>maturity</u> that he 'sulked' all the way home?

> **❝** *A black man's life ain't worth the life of a cowfly down here.* **❞**

Explore

What 'other way' do you think Mama has in mind to deal with the Wallaces?

On their journey home, Hammer <u>frightens</u> Mama and Big Ma by his talk of burning the Wallace store. Hammer's <u>impetuous</u> character cannot resist the temptation of getting one up on the Wallace family when they meet at the bridge. As an ex-soldier of World War I, Hammer's victory over the Wallaces at Soldiers Bridge is perhaps fitting – and an <u>omen</u> for the future – but Mama knows that one day they will have to pay for it. Hammer's victory will be all the more galling for the Wallaces because the right-of-way rule seems to be regularly broken if black families are on the bridge first; and because they mistook him for Harlan Granger, who seems to occupy top position in the local pecking order of importance, while we already know that 'nigras' are at the bottom.

Uncover the plot

Delete two of the three alternatives given, to find the correct plot.

1   The children learn from Mama/Mr Wallace/T.J. that the night men have burnt/tarred and feathered/beaten Mr Tatum after he accused the preacher/Mr Granger/Mr Barnett of being a liar.

2   T.J. cheats in a test at school but Stacey/Cassie/Mama ends up getting the blame. Mr Morrison breaks up the resulting fight between T.J. and Little Man/Stacey/Cassie.

3   The children are taken to visit Mr Tatum/Mr Berry/Mr Morrison to see his injuries. After visiting the market at Vicksburg/Jackson/Strawberry, Big Ma calls to see Mr Barnett/Mr Jamison/Mr Granger.

4   Mama tells Cassie how her ancestors originally came from Africa/Alabama/Arkansas and Uncle Hammer gives Stacey an early Christmas present of a book/a dog/a coat.

Who? What? Why? Where? How?

1   What was Little Man's greatest fear about being tarred and feathered?

2   Who gets a beating for protecting T.J.?

3   Whose two daughters died when they were young?

4   Where does Cassie experience the cruellest day in her life?

5   How is the right of way supposed to work at Soldiers Bridge, and what often happens instead?

More about people

1   Who says 'I already know what I am!', and to whom?

2   What is the relationship between Uncle Hammer and David Logan?

3   In which part of the world were Big Ma's parents, Papa Luke and Mama Rachel, both born?

4   'What we give them is not respect but fear'. Who says this to whom, and who are they talking about?

5   Against whom does Harlan Granger still hold a grudge because he sold two hundred acres of land to the Logans?

Chapters 7–9

Chapter 7

> ❝*I ain't got the coat*❞

Explore

How do you react to the reasons which Stacey gives for parting with the coat? What evidence is there to show that Stacey already knows he has been a fool?

Uncle Hammer's reaction to the news about the coat is much more frightening than the children would have expected from their father. The placing of this incident just before the arrival of Papa is not accidental – what effect is achieved by this arrangement? (Think about the contrasting characters of Papa and Hammer.)

> ❝*'O Papa!' I cried. 'I knew it was you!'*❞

The celebrations, when Papa returns as usual at Christmas, are vividly described and emphasise the happy, warm and loving home which the Logans share. As they gather together 'in the heart of the house' to share food, companionship and fond memories, their comfort, security and happiness contrast strongly with the unhappiness caused by the discrimination and hostility which some of the white community direct at black families, and which has been a feature of the last few chapters. It is this 'other' atmosphere which surfaces again when Jeremy arrives.

> ❝*They come down like ghosts that Christmas of seventy-six.*❞

A change of mood occurs as the evening wears on when Mr Morrison reminisces – almost to himself – about his memories of the past. The contrast with the Logans' memories is very strong. Why does Taylor have the characters talk at this time in 'hushed' voices? Think of other kinds of occasion when people might talk like this. Look carefully at Mr Morrison's first few words for a clue.

Text commentary

> **Hammer, you go to burning and we'll have nothing.**

Cassie wakens in the night from her evil dreams of a hell of flames and night men to <u>overhear</u> the adults discussing what can be done about the Wallace store. Notice how often Taylor uses this same 'overhearing' device to allow the reader to learn something they otherwise might not. This clever technique also emphasises the often <u>scary</u> <u>mood</u>; the novel is full of terrible deeds, or veiled threats – many events are only hinted at by characters, some of which are never to be spoken of at all, while others may be discussed only in secret or in low voices.

Explore

Which thing that Stacey does is never to be spoken of, and which thing does Papa do which is treated in the same way?

> **'Books!' cried Little Man on Christmas morning.**

The presents of books stresses the importance of education in the Logan household, and is a reminder of Mama's profession – but notice the <u>difference</u> between this occasion and the time at the school when books were given out. How was the sort of education the school books were intended to give <u>very</u> <u>different</u> to what the children will learn from these? To help you with this, look at Papa's comments about these treasured Christmas gifts. If you have yourself read any of the books which the children receive, you should be able to see that they all have something in common with the <u>values</u> which the children's parents are teaching them as they <u>grow</u> <u>up</u>.

> **Jeremy nodded and stepped hesitantly inside.**

Jeremy's visit is <u>uncomfortable</u> for almost everyone. Cassie's tactless outburst about Jeremy's gifts, and Mama's comment about her mouth, remind us that Cassie often speaks first and

thinks later. On what other occasion does Cassie's 'mouth' get her into trouble? Notice that Jeremy's gift is something he has made himself – what does this, and his comment 'it ain't much', tell you about the <u>sincerity of his friendship</u> for Stacey? What present have the Logan children given Jeremy?

Stacey rejects T.J.'s nasty comments about his present from Jeremy because he now has T.J.'s measure and can see that T.J. is <u>envious</u>. Stacey now realises that Jeremy would be a better friend. Papa's view of friendship between blacks and whites is <u>realistic</u> but <u>depressing</u>. However, look carefully at the reasons Papa gives for his belief, because later on we see that he may be wrong – think about what Mr Jamison does.

The children are punished for visiting the Wallace store – 'Papa never forgot anything'. Unpleasant though the beating is, why do the children prefer this kind of punishment to the tongue-lashing of Uncle Hammer?

❝I'll back the credit.❞

Following Big Ma's visit to his office in Strawberry, Mr Jamison has called with the papers to <u>transfer</u> the <u>ownership</u> of the land from her to her two sons. Unexpectedly, Mr Jamison offers to back the credit of families who wish to boycott the Wallace store, because he knows that if the Logans do so they can only offer their land as security. Notice that nobody challenges his assertion that if they did this they would lose the land – what unspoken understanding do they all have? (If the Logans put their land up as security think about what Harlan Granger would certainly do.) Mr Jamison is a lawyer with a <u>high regard for justice</u>; how does this explain why he and his wife have made this offer? Notice what he says about the Wallaces.

> **❝You plan on getting this land, you're planning on the wrong thing.❞**

The visit of Mr Jamison is swiftly followed by one from Harlan Granger. A clue to Uncle Hammer's dedication to their <u>ownership</u> of the land is given when we see that it is he who swiftly responds to Harlan Granger's threat about the loan with 'Ain't gonna lose it'. Hammer will later sell all he owns, even the car which so clearly irritates Harlan Granger, to back the loan. Papa says nothing until the end, letting Hammer keep goading Harlan Granger with the truth. Harlan Granger is obviously not used to being spoken to in this forthright and honest way, as we can see from his <u>'harsh'</u> voice and the way his face 'paled'. In contrast, Papa's voice is 'very quiet, very distinct, very sure', and he 'impaled' their visitor with his stare. We may feel that Mr Jamison was right and that the Logans cannot win. We may even agree that all Papa can do is 'want these children to know we tried'. But if Harlan Granger had been so sure of victory, would he have bothered to come to the Logans to try to make them change their minds?

Chapter 8

> **❝God wants all his children to do what's right.❞**

The last two chapters have been about people's thoughts and plans. The action of the book now resumes with Cassie's <u>revenge</u> on 'Miz' Lillian Jean. She gets good advice from Papa, who treats her like an adult when he advises her that it is up to her to decide what things in life she cannot <u>back down on</u>. Papa's comment also explains Stacey's earlier caution about the wrecking of the bus – whatever Cassie does, there must be no come-back from Mr Simms. Look how his comment that people have to have self-respect also explains Mr Jamison's reasons for

Explore

Whose words do you hear echoed from a previous occasion here? (Hint: it followed a fight.) Do you think Stacey guesses what's going on?

offering to back their credit. Papa's words are an echo of Cassie's ironic comment to Lillian Jean 'that's what I'm gonna do from now on. Just what I gotta.' Later, following her beating at Cassie's hands, it is clear that Lillian Jean never understood what hit her. From being someone who blurts out inappropriate comments, Cassie has now become someone who can hold her tongue — even in the face of outrage from her younger brothers and sneers from T.J. But notice Stacey's comment: 'This here thing's between Cassie and Lillian Jean…'

> ❝ *'She did it on purpose!' T.J. accused, a nasty scowl twisting his face.* ❞

T.J. flees after being caught cheating by Mama. The visit of the school board seems unconnected at the time, but later we learn that T.J. is responsible for this, and for Mama being fired as a result. Again, we witness the classroom scene through the eyes of Cassie, who is watching when she should be elsewhere. Significantly, two of the neighbourhood's biggest bigots — Harlan Granger and Kaleb Wallace — accuse Mama of doing wrong by teaching the truth about slavery as opposed to the distorted version of events written in the 'white' books approved by the Board of Education.

Taylor carefully avoids stereotyping all whites in the novel as racist and all blacks as good. Notice how Mr Wellever, the principal, gives her no support — like Miss Crocker he also, perhaps, regards Mama as a 'maverick'.

The day, which had begun with a victory for Cassie, ends with a defeat for Mama, underlining how vulnerable they are to the likes of Mr Granger. But Mama and the family take this with dignity. Mr Morrison offers to find work, and Papa says they will plant more cotton. Papa explains to the children the size of the sacrifice that Mama has had to make for her belief in justice.

On several occasions Big Ma, Mama and Papa go down to the pasture, or to the trees, when they want to think. Under what kind of circumstances do they do this, and why are the pasture or the press appropriate places for them to go? If this seems a difficult point, carefully re-read what Big Ma says in Chapter 4 about what the land means to her.

> ❝ *Y'all can't just turn on me just 'cause—* ❞

When the truth comes out about T.J.'s part in Mama being sacked, Stacey does not beat him as Little Man expects. Stacey has <u>learned</u> that there are worse punishments. This is an important moment in the story and is skilfully handled by Taylor. There is <u>dramatic</u> <u>irony</u> in what Stacey says, because his prophetic remark is true in a way he does not himself appreciate. We know that at the end of the book 'what he got coming to him is worse than a beating'.

When he gets back to school T.J. is <u>shunned</u> by the other students for what he has done. He is astonished by this. Which other character has reacted similarly to getting their come-uppance, and in what way are these two characters alike?

T.J. shouts after the children that he has better friends than them, white friends. But you should recall Papa's observations to Stacey on Christmas Day (when Jeremy called) that 'you see blacks hanging 'round with whites, they're headed for trouble'. Significantly, T.J.'s empty jibes 'faded into the wind'.

Explore

Why do you think that T.J.'s character has turned out like this, while the Logan children have turned out differently?

By now we see that T.J. is <u>untrustworthy</u> <u>and</u> <u>boastful</u>. He will <u>abuse</u> his family and friends and has no <u>respect</u> for anyone. He is completely <u>self-centred</u> and a <u>cheat</u>, and fails to make anything of his own education. He is also very jealous.

Text commentary

Chapter 9

> ## *I – I just meant we could still see each other.*

When Jeremy Simms wishes he could see the children more often, the inferior education of blacks is again emphasised by the much shorter school year they have. Stacey cannot understand why Jeremy does not like 'his own kin', but Cassie can. This underlines the <u>difference</u> between the <u>warm</u> and <u>loving</u> Logan family and that of the Simms or Wallaces. Jeremy's brothers Melvin and R.W. are obviously <u>taking advantage</u> of T.J., whom they regard as a figure of fun. Like Cassie, we probably cannot imagine that T.J. is 'dumb' enough not to know this, but Mama explains the real reason for T.J.'s behaviour. We have seen Mama's <u>keen insight</u> into the character of others before – remember her explanation to Cassie of why Mr Simms behaved that way he did in Strawberry. In their treatment of T.J., R.W. and Melvin are behaving very like their father, and for the same reasons. The Simms seem to need to <u>bully</u> <u>others</u> to bolster their own <u>poor</u> <u>self-esteem</u>.

> ## *'Good ole butter beans and cornbread!'*

Compare the meal the family have here with the festivities at Christmas. Although that was a special time, the <u>contrast</u> clearly shows how far they are having to tighten their belts – but Papa treats it as a feast. The visit of their loyal friend Mr Jamison hints at further <u>trouble</u> ahead and helps to build the <u>tension</u> in the story, together with Papa's 'gut feeling' that the trouble isn't over yet.

> ## *'Gotta go up to that store by tomorrow to show good faith.'*

Papa's <u>intuition</u> is proved correct when Mr Avery and Mr Lanier arrive to say that they have been bullied into shopping at the Wallace store again. Mr Granger says he will raise his share of

their crop to sixty per cent. In addition the Wallaces have <u>threatened</u> to call in their store debts and have those owing money put on the chain gang (a form of prison slave-labour where men were chained together in teams to work in harsh conditions on roads, railways, etc.). Papa is angered at Stacey's comments when the men have left. He explains that Stacey was 'born blessed' with ownership of land and that if he had not been he would, like families such as the Laniers and the Averys, 'cry out for it while you try to survive'. Cassie's crying for the land at the end of the novels is, like the incident here, another reminder of the meaning of the book's title and the central importance of <u>land ownership</u>. Notice how, later on, Papa's words to Cassie echo her own comment to Lillian Jean in Chapter 8: 'We keep doing what we gotta...'

Papa decides to continue to make the trip to Vicksburg and has included Stacey because he wants him to learn to take care of things, to grow up 'strong... not a fool like T.J.' Mama emphasises the importance of education when she says that Stacey has 'more brains and learning than that'. Again, we hear this conversation via the eavesdropping Cassie.

Explore

Mama and Papa have very differing views about how good a parent to T.J. Mr Avery is being. Which of them do you think is right?

> ❝*it began to rain, a hard, swelling summer rain*❞

As Papa, Stacey and Mr Morrison are due to return from Vicksburg, it begins to rain. The rumbling thunder <u>foreshadows</u> the events to come and the conversation in the Logan household becomes increasingly <u>tense</u> as the return of the wagon becomes overdue. The household has become the centre of a storm in several senses, and when Papa returns, shot and with a broken leg, it is clear that Stacey has seen more <u>growing up</u> than Papa had in mind. Their wagon was sabotaged by two boys (the Simms, perhaps?) in Vicksburg and during their return in the storm they were <u>attacked</u> in the dark while fixing it. Papa was shot and the wagon rolled over his leg, breaking it. The family's guardian angel, the giant Mr Morrison, faced their three attackers and badly injured two of them. It is clear that the attackers were the Wallaces. Stacey's too-quick denial of his brother's fear that their father will die shows how <u>frightening</u> he found the experience.

> ❝ *All the questions had been answered, yet we feared* ❞

Harlan Granger has had Mama sacked (with the unwitting help of T.J.) and the boycott of the store has largely collapsed following <u>threats</u> from Granger and the Wallaces. But the Wallaces have paid a high price for trying to get even with the Logans – one of them almost certainly has a broken back, another a broken arm, and they have been humiliated by being defeated in spite of having firearms and outnumbering Mr Morrison three to one. The Logans have also paid a high price. The <u>loss</u> of Mama's salary has <u>jeopardised</u> their ability to pay the mortgage on the land – opening up the threat of a take-over from Harlan Granger. And now Papa has almost been killed and will not be able to work on the railroad because of his broken leg, further <u>endangering</u> <u>their</u> <u>future</u> and their <u>ownership</u> <u>of</u> <u>the</u> <u>land</u>.

Uncover the plot
Delete two of the three alternatives given, to find the correct plot.

1   After Christmas dinner the children receive a surprise visit from Jeremy Simms/Mr Granger/Uncle Hammer, who has bought gifts.

2   Big Ma signs over the land to her two sons and Mr Granger/Mr Jamison/Mr Hollenbeck offers to back the credit of local families who wish to shop in Vicksburg.

3   Kaleb Wallace/Harlan Granger/Mr Andersen calls and threatens the family with the loss of their land if they continue to cause him trouble.

4   Stacey/Cassie/T.J. is caught cheating again in the examinations but gains revenge by getting Mama/Miss Crocker/Mr Wellever fired.

5   Papa/Mr Morrison/Mr Jamison is shot and his leg broken in a fight with the Wallaces one night, returning from shopping in Strawberry/Jackson/Vicksburg.

Who? What? Why? Where? How?

1   What, according to Mr Morrison, were 'breeded stock'?

2   How old was Mr Morrison when his parents died?

3   Who would prefer to deal with the Wallaces by burning them out?

4   What presents did the children receive on Christmas day?

5   According to Mr Jamison, what is it that Harlan Granger absolutely will not permit?

6   What changes occur in Mama's baking style after she is fired?

Who is this?

1   Who said that a man should not blame others for his own stupidity?

2   Who accuses the Averys and the Laniers of behaving like scared jackrabbits?

3   Who got so sick he couldn't discipline his son?

4   Who says 'It's m-my fault his leg's busted'?

5   Who stole watermelons from Mr Ellis, and when?

6   Who had a grudging respect for Mr Jamison and why?

Chapters 10–12

Chapter 10

> **I'm well enough to know there's not much left.**

Although times are obviously hard, Papa is <u>reluctant</u> to ask Hammer for money because this would mean telling him about how Papa was attacked. Papa knows that Hammer's <u>temper</u> could then cause even more <u>serious problems</u>. Taylor is at pains to show us that her characters are rounded people – see how Papa, still recovering from his injuries, says he would dearly love to whip the Wallaces. It is clear to Cassie, who is listening as usual, that even her mild-mannered father has to work hard to live up to his own <u>high</u> <u>standards</u>.

> **he lifted the truck in one fluid, powerful motion**

Explore

On what other occasion has a white character 'paled' when confronted by others in the black community who have a measured determination not to be bullied?

It tells us a lot about the <u>character</u> of whites like Kaleb Wallace that even though it was his family which carried out the cowardly attack on Papa, he is the one who feels that he has been <u>wronged</u>. He is a <u>cowardly</u> man unless backed by a crowd and a loaded gun. He is speechless and pales with fear when he thinks he might be attacked, but instead Mr Morrison uses his phenomenal strength to gently lift the truck out of the way. Notice how Mr Morrison checks to make sure there is no gun in the truck.

> **the simplest thing to do would be to tell the sheriff and have them put in jail**

Cassie finds the complicated way of things <u>confusing</u>, but Mama explains why it is safer for them not to make a fuss about the

attack of the Wallaces. The Wallaces and other like-minded whites will now be at their most <u>dangerous</u>, because until now they have been used to getting their own way all the time. Mama points out that these are now dangerous times.

Explore

Why do you think Jeremy pretend's that he can see the Logan place from his tree? What does Jeremy's tree-home tell you about how comfortable he feels with his own family?

Jeremy is always offering <u>friendship</u>, without any strings attached. Notice here how he takes rejection in his stride and is never put off for long. He tells the astonished children about how he has built his bedroom up a tree.

> **❝The bank called up the note.❞**

Papa correctly sees the <u>malicious</u> hand of Harlan Granger in the bank's sudden demand that the loan be <u>repaid</u> <u>in</u> <u>full</u> – even though, legally, the mortgage gives them four more years to pay it off. This is evidence of Harlan's need to show them 'where they stand in the scheme of things'.

> **❝the annual revival began.❞**

The celebrations which accompany the annual church revival form a powerful <u>contrast</u> to the troubles and aggression surrounding the black community. These occasions are a celebration of the <u>spiritual</u> <u>unity</u> of the larger black family to which they all belong, a time of sharing and of hope in spite of their struggles. Significantly, T.J. attends the revival as an <u>outcast</u>, while Hammer appears as a saving angel with the money the family needs.

> **❝It's gonna storm all right… but it may not come till late on over in the night.❞**

Papa's words here are <u>prophetic</u>, for the climax of the book's action is drawing rapidly closer. As the storm gathers, T.J. arrives, accompanied by R.W. and Melvin Simms – two <u>symbols</u> of all that threatens the black community. His <u>shallow</u> <u>values</u> are

Text commentary

emphasised by the way he thinks that the important things in life are having fancy new clothes (remember Stacey's coat?), and being given the pearl-handled pistol. It becomes clear that the Simms brothers have only come with T.J. as part of an agreement that he will then do something they want.

Symbolically, the Logan children <u>turn their backs</u> on these 'white devils' and go into church. T.J. is left, <u>lonely and pathetic</u>, stranded in the darkness between his own people in the church and the insistent hooting of the horn of the white boys' truck. Fatefully, T.J. yet again makes the <u>wrong</u> decisions.

Chapter 11

❝ *Roll of thunder, hear my cry* **❞**

Explore

Notice the significant use of the word 'chant' to describe his singing of the song from which the book gets its title. Why has Mildred Taylor used this word, do you think?

The night is full of distant thunder as Mr Morrison sits as usual, watching and waiting, and chants his song of <u>defiance</u>. His behaviour is another of those things which Cassie knows are never spoken of, although she is certain she knows why he watches and waits. Mr Morrison knows that, like the approaching storm, events are building rapidly <u>to a climax</u>. He waits in the certain knowledge that <u>trouble is coming</u>. Look carefully at the words of the song. Consider what else is usually chanted, and what this tells you about Mr Morrison's role in the story.

❝ *The door swung open and T.J. slipped inside.* **❞**

During the night a <u>distressed</u> T.J. arrives. He has been <u>beaten</u> and <u>threatened</u> by his white 'friends' R.W. and Melvin Simms. He tells the children he is afraid to go home because his father will throw him out, and that the Simms have threatened him if he

tells about the night's events. We learn about the robbery and how the Simms have cleverly duped T.J. Notice that although T.J. is not the one who has committed the violence against the Barnetts, the Simms covered their faces so that they will be taken for blacks. So while they remain unknown, T.J.'s face was plainly visible and because of the pistol he is the one with evidence which <u>incriminates</u> him. After the robbery the Simms have gone to the pool hall, probably to fix up an alibi, and left the beaten T.J. in the wagon. He has made his painful way home, avoiding the Simms' place out of fear of further beatings. T.J. has <u>realised</u> <u>far</u> <u>too</u> <u>late</u> that his only true friend has been Stacey.

> **❝*Thunder crashed against the corners of the world.*❞**

The thunder, like a wild animal stalking its prey, is 'creeping closer now, rolling angrily over the forest depths and bringing the lightning with it', as the children take the injured T.J. home and watch him climb into the house through a side window. The 'lightning' is indeed approaching, as half a dozen vehicles suddenly appear and flood the unsuspecting Avery house with their headlights. An <u>angry</u> <u>mob</u> <u>of</u> <u>men</u> – including R.W. and Melvin Simms – storm the house and drag the family out and severely attack them. They have come for T.J. and their savagery upsets the Logan children. But Stacey knows that for their own safety they must not be discovered. The Simms brothers have pinned everything on T.J. who, stupidly, still has the pistol on him.

Why is there 'an embarrassed silence' when Mr Jamison arrives? Look at how he reacts to the men's threats. Who else reacts to threats in a calm, unruffled manner, and do the two men have anything else in common?

The behaviour of the sheriff, who acts 'as if he would rather not be here at all' tells us where his <u>loyalties</u> <u>lie</u> and <u>contrasts</u> with that of the <u>brave</u> Mr Jamison. The sheriff has no words of his own to speak, he is only a messenger for Harlan Granger, who obviously <u>does</u> <u>not</u> <u>care</u> what happens so long as it is not on his land. Notice that although the sheriff <u>represents</u> <u>the</u> <u>law</u>, Mr Jamison <u>represents</u> <u>justice</u>. We have already seen, on many occasions, that the two <u>are</u> <u>not</u> <u>the</u> <u>same</u>.

Mr Jamison rushes to defend T.J. from immediate hanging. As the mob talk of hanging Papa and Mr Morrison also, Cassie leaves Stacey at the Avery house, takes her younger brothers and agrees to go home and get Papa. As they make their way home the thunder 'crashed' against the corners of the world'. We do not see T.J. again.

Chapter 12

"Papa stared out as a bolt of lightning splintered the night"

When Papa hears about what is taking place at the Averys', he swiftly moves to help, but Mama <u>pleads</u> with him not to use the gun. As Papa looks out into the night the lightning again splits the sky – a <u>symbol</u> of the <u>violence</u> <u>erupting</u> all around them. Papa's mysterious reply 'Perhaps…' gives us no clue as to how he will resolve the difficult situation. His <u>determination</u> is shown when he again says that he will do what he has to do, a phrase which, as we have seen, sums up the courage of the Logans.

Text commentary

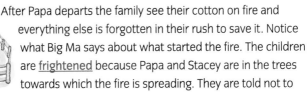

> **“You mean you been out there fighting that fire?”**

After Papa departs the family see their cotton on fire and everything else is forgotten in their rush to save it. Notice what Big Ma says about what started the fire. The children are <u>frightened</u> because Papa and Stacey are in the trees towards which the fire is spreading. They are told not to go out, and Mama and Big Ma go to help put out the fire. Later, Stacey arrives. He has been concerned about them and has been with his father <u>fighting the fire</u> like everyone else. Jeremy does not realise why all the men were already there, but he tells them that they have all been fighting the fire. The knowledge that they all <u>depend on the land</u> has put other things <u>aside</u> while everyone co-operates to help to save the crops and forests.

> **“the stalks were singed, and the fine gray ash of the fire lay thick upon them”**

Explore

Notice how everyone – from the bigoted Harlan Granger to the vicious Kaleb Wallace – is helping, 'each oblivious of the other'.

Following the sudden heavy downpour, the fire is put out and the children witness the charred and desolate landscape. The <u>destruction</u> of the land echoes what the mob were trying to do to their <u>community</u>. The children find a 'flood' of people working to put out the last of the fire.

> **“I wanna know what happened over there.”**

Stacey and Mama know what Papa did – he set the fire <u>deliberately</u>, sacrificing some of their cotton crop, to save the situation. When Cassie asks Stacey why Mr Morrison arrived at the Averys' place without Papa, he deliberately offers a reason which they all see cannot be true. Cassie shows how much she has <u>matured</u> by voicing her concern about whether they will have enough money to pay the taxes –

Text commentary

she sees that the land not only <u>supports</u> <u>and</u> <u>feeds</u> them, but that it is a <u>symbol</u> of <u>black</u> <u>freedom</u> <u>from</u> <u>oppression</u>, and of <u>hope</u> <u>for</u> <u>the</u> <u>future</u>.

Stacey tells the others about Mr Jamison's bravery in stopping the mob, at risk to his own life, and how Harlan Granger intervened and ordered T.J. to be turned over to Mr Jamison only when his own land was at risk. When Mr Jamison is overheard talking to Papa and Mr Morrison, we hear that Mr Barnett has died – so the charge against T.J. is likely to be one of <u>murder</u>.

> ❝ *folks thinking that lightning struck that fence of yours and started the fire...* ❞

Mr Jamison has obviously <u>realised</u> what has really happened to start the fire, but he leaves this unspoken, advising Papa to stay clear of things for a while. Cassie realises that Papa started the fire, but that this is another of those 'known and unknown things, never to be spoken' and she tells us that her glance at Stacey revealed that she 'knew, and understood the meaning of what I knew'.

> ❝ *I cried for T.J. For T.J. and the land.* ❞

T.J.'s earlier <u>ominous</u> comment that he would <u>sell</u> <u>his</u> <u>life</u> for the pearl-handled pistol seems to be coming true, as Papa's answers to the children's questions make clear. Papa says that while it may have to be that way, 'it shouldn't be'. This is a central theme which runs through the novel. Cassie sees that T.J. is <u>unlikely</u> to get <u>justice</u> at his trial, and that even though it is almost 150 years after the American Constitution declared that all men were created <u>equal</u>, for many blacks this is still a <u>hope</u> for the <u>future</u>, not a present reality. She knows that the <u>struggle</u> <u>must</u> <u>go</u> <u>on</u>, but has learned how and when she should fight and when she should remain silent. She <u>understands</u> the importance of the land and her place in her inheritance. And she has learned to feel sorrow for the <u>sacrifices</u> that <u>dignity,</u> <u>self-respect</u> <u>and</u> <u>freedom</u> will continue to demand of them all.

Uncover the plot

Delete two of the three alternatives given, to find the correct plot.

1   Papa is leaving/getting better/getting worse but money is still tight, so Mr Morrison/Mama/Stacey is out looking for work.

2   Returning from helping Mr Avery/Mr Wiggins/Mr Granger, Mr Morrison meets Kaleb Wallace/Mr Jamison/Mr Barnett, who blocks the road with his truck.

3   After being involved in a robbery at the Barnett store, Jeremy/Stacey/T.J. is caught when his accomplices, the Simms/Avery/Granger brothers, turn him in.

4   In order to protect the family and the Averys from prosecution/the sheriff/hanging, Papa starts a fight/fire/party.

5   The tension is defused as everyone celebrates/ignores/deals with this, but Mama/Papa/Cassie weeps for the unfairness of events.

Who? What? Why? Where? How?

1   Why does Papa not want Uncle Hammer to find out that he is injured?

2   What is in the envelope which Mr Morrison brings back from strawberry?

3   How do fire and water between them avert two disasters?

4   Who suggests that the mob hang Papa and Mr Morrison?

5   What piece of evidence is produced to implicate T.J. in the robbery?

More about people

1   What happens to T.J. after the fire?

2   Who says, 'Y'all decide to hold court out here tonight?' and to whom?

3   What is the real meaning of the message which the sheriff brings from Mr Granger?

4   'Since when did you start worrying about taxes?' Who says this and to whom?

5   Why do people think the fire started in the cotton field, and how did it really start?

- To prepare for an exam, you should read the text through *at least twice*, preferably *three times*. In order to answer an exam question on it you need to know it very well.

- If you are studying the text for an 'open book' exam, make sure that you take your copy of the text with you. However, do not rely on it too much – you haven't got time. If you are not allowed to take the text in with you, you will need to memorise brief quotations.

- Read all the questions carefully before deciding which one you are going to answer. Choose the question that best allows you to demonstrate your understanding and personal ideas.

- Make sure that you understand exactly what the question is asking you to do.

- Plan your answer carefully before starting to write your essay (see page 70).

- Always begin your answer with a short introduction which gives an overview of the topic. Use your plan to help keep you focused on the question as you write the essay. Try to leave enough time to write a brief conclusion.

- Remember to use the **point–quotation–comment** approach, where you make a point, support it with a short quotation, then comment on it. Use short and relevant quotations – do not waste time copying out chunks of the text.

- Make sure that you know how much time you have for each question and stick to it.

- Leave enough time at the end of the exam to check your work through carefully and correct any spelling or other mistakes that you have made.

- Timing is not as crucial for coursework essays, so this is your chance to show what you can really do, without having to write under pressure. Do not leave your coursework essays until the last minute though. If you have to rush your work it is unlikely to be the best you can produce.

- Coursework allows you to go into more detail and develop your ideas in greater depth. The required length of assignments varies, and your teacher will advise you on this.

- If you have a choice of title, make sure you choose one which you are interested in and which gives you the chance to develop your ideas.

- Plan your essay carefully (see page 70). Refer to your plan and the essay title as you write, to check that you are staying on course.

- Use quotations in your essay, but beware of using them **too frequently** or making them **too long**. Often, the best quotes are just one or two words or short phrases. Make sure that they are relevant to the points that you are making.

- If your topic requires it, use appropriate background information and put the text in a cultural and historical context. Remember, though, that the text itself should be at the centre of your essay.

- Include a short conclusion which sums up the key points of your ideas.

- Do not copy any of your essay from another source, e.g. other notes or the Internet. This is called plagiarism, and it is very serious if the exam board find that you have done this.

- If you have used sources, list them in a bibliography at the end of the essay.

- If you are allowed to word process your essay, it will be easier to make changes and to re-draft it.

Key quotations

> ❝ *Look out there, Cassie girl. All that belongs to you. You ain't never had to live on nobody's place but your own and as long as I live and the family survives, you'll never have to.* ❞

These lines are spoken to Cassie by her father at the beginning of the novel. They can be used to illustrate how the land is very important to Cassie and her family.

> ❝ *Whose little nigger is this!' bellowed Mr Barnett. Everybody in the store turned and stared at me. 'I ain't nobody's little nigger!' I screamed, angry and humiliated.* ❞

These lines are spoken by Cassie and Mr Barnett, the owner of the store in Strawberry. White people have been served before Cassie even though she was being served first, and she has objected. The quotation can be used to show how the black people are constantly subjected to racist and unequal treatment at the hands of some white people.

> ❝ *Baby, we have no choice of what color we're born or who our parents are or whether we're rich or poor. What we do have some choice over what we make of our lives once we're here.* ❞

These lines are spoken by Mama when she is comforting Cassie about the injustices that black people have to suffer at the hands of the whites. The quotation can be used to show how Cassie is affected by such treatment and the attitude of dignified independence that her mother tries to encourage in her.

> *"Visions of night riders and fire mixed in a cauldron of fear awakened me long before dawn."*

These lines describe Cassie waking from a bad dream. They can be used to show how Cassie is troubled by the events that are happening and the situation her family is in.

> *"Cassie, there'll be a whole lot of things you ain't gonna wanna do, but you'll have to do in this life just so you can survive."*

These lines are spoken to Cassie by Papa when he is giving her advice about how to handle the Lillian Jean situation. The quotation can be used to illustrate how Cassie learns about life and develops through the course of the novel.

> *"I cried for T.J. For T.J. and the land."*

These are Cassie's closing lines in the novel and sum up her feelings. The quotation can be used to show how she knows that T.J. will not get a fair trial at the hands of the white people. It also shows that she has grown and developed throughout the course of the novel and now understands the importance of the land to them all and to who they are as people, and recognises the struggle that they face to be free and independent.

Key quotations

Exam questions

1. *Discuss Taylor's presentation of the character of Cassie, exploring the ways in which she changes during the course of the novel.*

2. *Write a comparison of Uncle Hammer and Mr Morrison.*

3. *How is the idea of 'friendship' important in* Roll of Thunder, Hear My Cry?

4. *Remind yourself of the last section of* Roll of Thunder, Hear My Cry, *beginning 'I sat very still, listening to the soft sounds of the early morning...' to the end of the novel. How effective do you find this ending?*

5. *Explore the different ways in which prejudice is important in the novel.*

6. *Do you think that T.J. gets what he deserves in the novel?*

7. *What does* Roll of Thunder, Hear My Cry *have to say about loyalty and self-respect?*

8. *How is the idea of land ownership important in* Roll of Thunder, Hear My Cry? *Why is it so important to David Logan and his family?*

9. *Discuss the roles and importance of the following three characters: Mr Morrison; Wade Jamison; Jeremy Timms.*

10. *Compare the characters of Big Ma and Mrs Logan.*

11. *How is the setting and social background important to the overall effect of* Roll of Thunder, Hear My Cry?

12. *What is the significance of the incident involving the school books, and how does it contribute to the overall impact of the novel?*

13. *What have you learned about attitudes to education and 1930s' Mississippi from the novel?*

14 *Through an examination of **two** or **three** incidents from the novel, discuss what attitudes and values Mama wants to convey to her children and how she does this.*

15 *Read again the passage from near the end of Chapter 4, after Mama Logan has taken the children to see the Berrys, starting 'After we were on the main road again, having ridden in thoughtful silence…' to ' "Everyone knows they did it, and the Wallaces even laugh about it, but nothing was ever done" '.*

*Black people are treated very badly in the novel and the law does not protect them. Do you agree? Refer to **at least two** episodes in the novel in your answer.*

16 *In what ways do the Logans struggle hard to keep their land? You may wish to consider:*

- *the history of land ownership in the Logan household*

- *the working lives of the Logans*

- *Big Ma signing over land to her sons*

- *Papa setting fire to the land at the end of the novel.*

Planning an essay

In order to write an effective essay, you need to approach your task in an organised way. You need to **plan** your essay carefully before beginning to write. This will help you to achieve a higher grade.

- The first thing to do is read the question carefully to make sure that you fully understand it, then highlight key words.

- You will need to make notes on the topic in order to start preparing your ideas. You can do this in various ways, such as making a list of key points, or creating a spidergram or a mind map.

- One advantage of using mind maps or spidergrams is that they help you to create links between the various points you make. Put the title of the essay in the middle of a page and add your points around it. You can then draw lines to connect up various points or ideas, linking them in a clear, visual way.

- If you wish, you can colour code your ideas, or even add pictures or symbols if that helps you to think about your ideas more clearly.

- Since mind maps and spidergrams are a way of charting your knowledge, they are also an excellent revision aid. You could work through a number of essay titles in this way. (See some examples of spidergrams on the following pages.)

- In the planning stage of your essay it is also a good idea to jot down some useful quotations. These should be kept brief and to the point, and can be added to your spidergram.

- It can also be useful to plan what you are going to write in each paragraph of your essay. You can number the branches on your spidergram, so that you are clear about the order of your points. This will help you to structure your work more effectively.

- Remember that you are much more likely to write an effective essay if you do some planning before you start to write it.

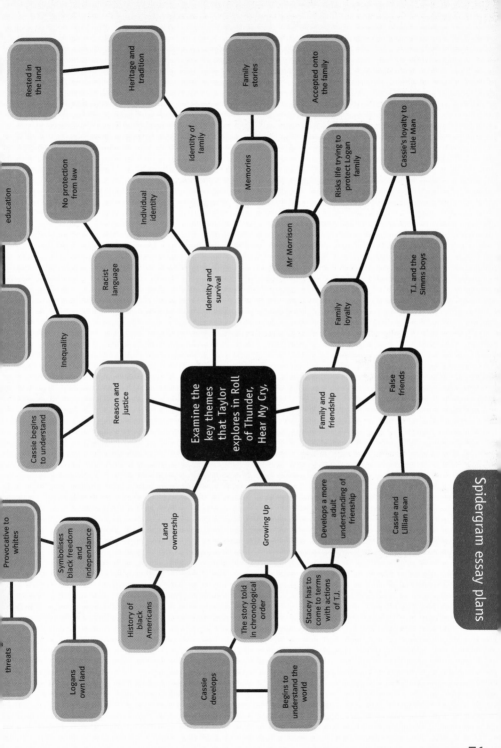

Spidergram essay plans

Examine the key themes that Taylor explores in Roll of Thunder, Hear My Cry.

- Identity and survival
  - Individual identity
  - Identity of family
    - Heritage and tradition
      - Rested in the land
    - Memories
    - Family stories

- Reason and justice
  - Racist language
    - No protection from law
    - Inequality
    - education
  - Cassie begins to understand

- Family and friendship
  - Family loyalty
    - Mr Morrison
      - Risks life trying to protect Logan family
      - Accepted onto the family
    - Cassie's loyalty to Little Man
    - T.J. and the Simms boys
  - False friends
    - Develops a more adult understanding of friendship
    - Cassie and Lillian Jean

- Land ownership
  - Symbolises black freedom and independance
    - Provocative to whites
    - threats
  - Logans own land
  - History of black Americans

- Growing Up
  - Stacey has to come to terms with actions of T.J.
  - The story told in chronological order
  - Cassie develops
    - Begins to understand the world

71

Spidergram essay plans

Examine the presentation of the character of Cassie Logan

- **intelligent**
  - questions things
- **loyal**
  - protective instincts towards brother
  - stands by little man
- **learns how to take revenge**
  - learns about the nature of 'friendship'
    - TJ and the Simms
    - Lillian Jean
    - Jeremy Simms
- **begins to recognise injustices**
  - shop keeper
- **challenges authority**
  - tea boss
  - situation with boss
  - first 'protest' happens in school
- **protagonists of story**
  - nine years old
  - situation seen through her eyes
- **hain sense of identity**
- **growing up**
  - comes to recognise the value of the lamb
  - becoming aware of differences between herself or other children
    - differences based on colour
    - finds it difficult to accept
  - recognises she is forced to take second place to whites
    - humiliated in store
    - the adults cannot protect her

when T.J. held his eye as if he was hurt, then T.J. rammed into Stacey, and they both fell to the ground. The fight was stopped by huge, strong Mr Morrisson. This proves T.J. is a coward and can't take the effects of his actions. He doesn't care about others, even his so-called closest friend, Stacey. ✓

T.J. Avery is a tall, thin boy who wears patched clothes and this shows he is poor. He isn't very bright as he was kept down a year at school. He didn't wear shoes as he couldn't afford them. He is a year older than Stacey, as he had to repeat Stacey's year (Stacey is 12). I think others see T.J. Avery as a coward and a liar who can worm his way out of things easily (people like Cassie think this). But he is seen differently by adults because he sucks up to them ✓ and always gets others into trouble for what he does, so they don't see him as a troublemaker. Overall I think the best way to describe T.J. Avery is selfish, cowardly, a liar, he lacks confidence, he wants to impress, he's foolish and doesn't realise what his actions will do to someone. ✓

Examiner's comments

There is good focus on the question and a range of relevant points are made. Clear knowledge and evaluation of the character are shown and ideas are supported by references to the text. The essay is well-structured, but slang expressions such as 'big-mouthed' and 'took the mickey' should be avoided. Also try to avoid simply retelling the story.

Write a character study of one of the following: Cassie or Uncle Hammer or Mr Morrison or T.J.

Cassie is nine years old and is a young, but strong-minded girl. ✓ Cassie can be very quick tempered and fiery, especially towards her younger brothers. ✓ She is very independent ✓ and has a strong sense of justice. ✓ If she is treated unfairly she tries her hardest to get her own back. This is shown when she accidentally walks into Lillian-Jean at the store in Vicksburg. ✓ Mr Simms makes her get down in the road and apologise to Lillian-Jean. Cassie is very upset. After this she decides to lull Lillian-Jean into a false sense of security. Cassie offers to carry her books for her. During this time Lillian-Jean reveals many secrets about her family which, if they were spread around, would affect the Simms badly. ✓ One day, Cassie takes Lillian-Jean to a quiet place in the woods, pretending there is something she wants to show her. Cassie smashes Lillian-Jean's books on the ground. Lillian-Jean tries to make her pick them up, but Cassie refuses. They get into a fight and Cassie makes Lillian-Jean apologise for everything she and her family have done wrong. ✓

Cassie loves the outdoors, ✓ as is shown when she has to walk to school in her Sunday school dress and shoes: 'I tugged again at my collar and dragged my feet in the dust, allowing it to sift back into my socks and shoes like gritty red snow'. I hated the dress. And the shoes. There was little I could do in a dress, and as for shoes, they imprisoned freedom-loving feet accustomed to feel the warm earth.' ✓

When the bus for the white children drives past the Logan children, the bus driver swerves it towards them, making them dirty on numerous occasions. One wet day the Logan children, including Cassie, dig up part of the road and fill it with water. At the end of the day when the bus sets off it drops into the ditch and breaks down. The white children are forced to walk for a few months.

Stacey and the other Logan children think Cassie can be bad tempered, ✓ but most of the time she is very kind towards them. Her parents and grandma think she is a very active, fun-loving child.✓ She is well behaved and does as she is told, even when she doesn't agree with it. She will fight for her beliefs even if this comes at a price. She believes it is a small price to pay for equality. Cassie is bright and very proud of what she is. She values their land as a source of independence. She learns from every one of her encounters with the whites and racism. ✓

Examiner's comments

This a well-focused response in which the student makes a number of relevant points about Cassie. The response shows a good understanding of the plot and Cassie's role in it. The candidate is also aware of the different perceptions that other characters in the story have of Cassie and the ways in which she learns and develops throughout the novel. The response could have been improved further through the use of shorter, relevant textual references to support the well-made points.

Quick quiz answers

Quick quiz 1
Uncover the plot
1   brothers; Mississippi; grandmother
2   Crocker; Little Man; Cassie; discarded
3   slimy gully; Stacey
4   a hole; crashes

Who? What? Why? When? Where?
1   because the price of cotton dropped
2   because he got his brother punished for something which he himself did wrong
3   that he will beat them with a switch (a flexible twig or cane)
4   over by Smellings Creek
5   It was his idea to wreck the bus; so he thinks the night men are out, and the family at risk, because of him.

Character clues
1   T.J.'s brother, Claude
2   Mary Logan
3   Little Man
4   Mr Morrison
5   Cassie

Quick quiz 2
Uncover the plot
1   T.J.; tarred and feathered; Mr Barnett
2   Stacey; Stacey
3   Mr Berry; Strawberry; Mr Jamison
4   Africa; coat

Who? What? Why? Where? How?
1   that if it happened to them they would never get clean again
2   Stacey
3   Big Ma's
4   in Strawberry
5   Whoever is at the bridge first is supposed to have right of way, but often black families have to back off the bridge to give way to white.

More about people
1   Cassie, talking to Mr Barnett
2   they are brothers
3   in Mississippi
4   Mama says this to Cassie about white people like Mr Simms.
5   Mr Jamison

Quick quiz 3
Uncover the plot
1   Jeremy Simms
2   Mr Jamison
3   Harlan Granger
4   T.J.; Mama
5   Papa; Vicksburg

Who? What? Why? Where? How?
1   slaves bred together to produce more slaves for selling, especially after the government outlawed bringing any more slaves from Africa
2   barely six years old
3   Uncle Hammer
4   books, licorice, oranges, bananas and clothes
5   the idea that the Wallaces should be punished just as if they had killed a white man, because that would denote equality between blacks and whites
6   she uses less of the ingredients

Who is this?
1   Uncle Hammer
2   Stacey
3   Mr Avery
4   Stacey
5   Papa and Uncle Hammer, when
    they were young
6   Uncle Hammer, because he was
    honest about why even the
    whites who were sympathetic to
    the blacks wouldn't help them

Quick quiz 4
Uncover the plot
1   getting better; Mr Morrison
2   Mr Wiggins; Kaleb Wallace
3   T.J.; Simms
4   hanging; fire
5   deals; Cassie

Who? What? Why? Where? How?
1   because he does not want to
    risk Uncle Hammer's temper if
    he finds out what the Wallaces
    have done
2   a letter from the bank demanding
    immediate settlement of the loan
    on the land
3   The fire in the cotton field
    prevents the mob from hanging
    the Averys and the Logans
    and the rainstorm prevents
    the fire from destroying the
    forest and the other
    surrounding lands.
4   Kaleb and Thurston Wallace
5   the pearl-handed pistol

More about people
1   The sheriff and Mr Jamison take
    him to jail.
2   Mr Jamison makes this remark
    to the men who drag the Averys
    out of their home after the
    robbery at the Barnett store.
3   that Mr Granger does not really
    care what the men do to the
    Averys, or any other blacks,
    but that he will not be
    implicated by having it happen
    on his land
4   Mama says this to Cassie.
5   People think that lightning
    struck a fence and set it alight,
    but in fact Papa started the fire
    on purpose.

Page 18, Mildred Taylor, © Jack Ackerman. Reprinted by permission of Penguin Young Readers Group, a member of Penguin Group (USA) Inc. Page 20, scene, © Bettman/Corbis

First published 1994
Revised edition 2004

Letts Educational
Chiswick Centre
414 Chiswick High Road
London W4 5TF
Tel: 020 8996 3333

Text © Stewart Martin 1994
2004 edition revised by Steven Croft

Cover and text design by Hardlines Ltd., Charlbury, Oxfordshire.

Typeset by Letterpart Ltd., Reigate, Surrey.

Graphic illustration by Beehive Illustration, Cirencester, Gloucestershire.

Commissioned by Cassandra Birmingham

Editorial project management by Jo Kemp

Printed in Italy.

British Library Cataloguing in Publication Data. A CIP record of this book is available from the British Library.

ISBN 1 84315 318 1

Letts Educational is a division of Granada Learning, part of Granada plc.